Original title:
The Mirthful Maple

Copyright © 2025 Creative Arts Management OÜ
All rights reserved.

Author: George Mercer
ISBN HARDBACK: 978-1-80567-377-4
ISBN PAPERBACK: 978-1-80567-676-8

Shades of Joyful Leaves

Leaves dance like clowns in a whimsical show,
Twirling and spinning, putting on a glow.
They giggle and whisper, sharing a jest,
While the sun peeks in, enjoying their fest.

Boughs bent with chuckles, they'd sway to and fro,
Telling tales of squirrels who put on a row.
In shades of red, orange, and gold they gleam,
Creating a canvas of autumnal dream.

Dance of the Crimson Canopy

A canopy draped in crimson delight,
Looks down on dances from morning to night.
With each little breeze, the branches do sway,
As leaves share their secrets in a joyous ballet.

Boughs rustle softly, like friends at a feast,
As fungi giggle, and mushrooms are eased.
The earth chuckles back, a partner so dear,
In this theater of nature, spreading good cheer.

A Symphony of Golden Breezes

Golden breezes tickle and tease,
Turning the air into musical ease.
Each leaf takes a turn, like a star on the rise,
As sunlight beams down, sparking laughter in skies.

Rustling, they join the whimsical tune,
Playing maracas beneath the moon.
With every gust, a giggle they share,
In this vibrant world, where joy lingers in air.

Crimson Cheer on the Breeze

Leaves of red dance in the air,
Whispers of laughter, a playful flair.
Squirrels chase shadows, round and round,
Giggling softly, joy knows no bound.

Branches sway to a cheerful tune,
Birds join in, oh, what a swoon!
With every flutter, a chuckle grows,
Nature's giggle, everyone knows.

Lively Laughter in the Orchard

Fruit hangs low, a jester's grin,
Bees buzzing merrily, buzzing in.
Ripe apples tumble, rolling away,
Chasing each other, sweet game they play.

Cheeky chipmunks, in stripes so bright,
Steal a snack under soft twilight.
Their tiny paws, a tiny crime,
Makes the orchard chuckle each time.

Flickers of Folly Beneath the Boughs

Swaying branches, a leafy parade,
Rustling secrets, jokes never fade.
Caterpillars waltz in silly lines,
Spinning their stories like vintage wines.

Acorns tap dance, a percussion delight,
Creating giggles in soft twilight.
Underneath boughs, frolic and play,
Where laughter echoes, come what may.

Sun-Kissed Revelries

Golden rays tickle cheeky sprouts,
Sunshine giggles as the day shouts.
Shadow puppets dance on the ground,
In this merry realm, joy knows no bound.

Picnics erupt with spontaneous cheers,
As laughter spills, it banishes fears.
With each smile shared, the air's aglow,
In these sun-kissed moments, hearts overflow.

Golden Tapestry of Delight

In autumn's embrace, the leaves take flight,
Dancing with laughter in sunlight bright.
Whispers of joy in every sway,
Tickling the breeze, they play all day.

Beneath a tree, a squirrel spins round,
Gathering acorns from the ground.
He dons a cape of orange hues,
Nuts in pockets, he can't refuse.

A critter parade, all frolic and cheer,
Each little friend brings their own souvenir.
A feathered hat, a sunflower crown,
In this goofy revelry, joy's found.

As shadows stretch and twilight gleams,
The forest hums with playful dreams.
Each branch and twig joins in the fun,
Under the sky, the day is done.

Radiant Daydreams in the Forest

A funny fox with a jaunty gait,
Tripping on leaves, oh isn't fate great!
With each comical jump and twist,
He winks at nature, can't be missed.

Sunbeams bounce off golden crowns,
While chipmunks giggle and dance in gowns.
Fluffy tails wagging, a joyous sight,
In the sunlight, everything feels right.

Mushroom umbrellas dot the ground,
Where rabbits hop without a sound.
They pause and laugh, with noses twitch,
In this silly world, they all are rich.

Dreams of shadows chase the light,
As the moon peeks in, it's a delightful night.
With laughter carried on the breeze,
Nature's giggle brings hearts to ease.

The Ecstasy of Falling Leaves

Leaves tumble down, a carnival flight,
Playing tag in the soft sunlight.
They swirl and twirl, a wild ballet,
Nature's chuckles echo all day.

A gust of wind makes a quick dash,
Sending a jumble of colors to splash.
The world painted with giggling cheer,
As each leaf lands, "I'm finally here!"

In the woodland, laughter ignites,
Creatures delight in the playful sights.
A dance of shades, the trees sway low,
"Catch me if you can!" they seem to crow.

With every plop, a secret's shared,
In each rustling, the forest dared.
To join the fun, the chatter remains,
Of joyous bursts, like colorful canes.

Whimsical Roots of Joy

Underneath the ground, roots twist and twine,
They giggle together, so simply divine.
Talking jokes about the leaves up high,
Sharing secrets, oh me, oh my!

The next joke told sends shivers around,
As worms wiggle, creating a sound.
With laughter bursting up through the soil,
They push up daisies, oh what a toil!

A clumsy bear trips over a mound,
Rooty laughter is all around.
He chuckles back, "I'll dance through the muck,"
Wobbling on legs, oh what luck!

As seeds take flight on this joyful spree,
Roots grin wide, "Come join us, free!"
In this merry dance, life feels just right,
Whimsy abounds, from day to night.

Lush Laughter Among the Trees

In the woods, where whispers play,
Leaves dance in a wobbly way.
Squirrels giggle on a limb,
Chasing shadows, wild and grim.

A woodpecker's drum doth sound,
As laughter bounces all around.
Branches sway with joyful flair,
Tickling the breeze without a care.

A Tangle of Colors and Cheer

Red and gold in playful swirl,
Underneath, a joyful whirl.
A pumpkin rolls with a silly grin,
Clowning round in all his kin.

Each step a crunch, a sound so sweet,
Nature's laughter at our feet.
Maple's giggles, bright and bold,
Wrap us in a quilt of gold.

Darting Shadows of Delight

Squirrels dart with cheeky flair,
Hiding nuts with utmost care.
Leaves throw shadows on the ground,
In every cranny, joy is found.

A rustle here, a bounce, a leap,
Nature's secrets, softly keep.
Whispers tickle in the air,
As shadows play, we dance without a care.

Serendipitous Strolls Through Autumn

With every step, a crackling sound,
A treasure of laughter all around.
Twirling leaves with a twist and flick,
Nature's joke; it's quite the trick!

Each path we wander, heads held high,
Chasing giggles that float and fly.
In a world so fun and bright,
Tumbling leaves laugh with delight.

The Colorful Dance of Wind

In the breeze, leaves twirl and spin,
They play tag with squirrels, a raucous din,
Branches bend low, a boisterous bow,
Nature's jesters, stealing the show.

With laughter echoing through the trees,
They tease the flowers, 'Come dance with these!'
Petals whirl like confetti bright,
A party beneath the golden light.

The trunks sway gently, a happy crowd,
Join the ruckus, oh, how they're proud,
Each gust brings giggles, a playful tune,
Under the watch of a chuckling moon.

Swaying with Delight

Leaves toss and turn with giddy grace,
Their joyful jig charms every face,
Roots tap dance in the cool, soft earth,
Celebrating nature's cheerful mirth.

Branches reach out to hug the sky,
Waving to passersby up high,
In the sun's warm glow, they shimmy and sway,
A leafy ballet, come join their play!

Breezes carry giggles, soft and sweet,
Radiant colors in rhythmic beat,
As twiggy ballerinas spin so free,
Nature's own show, what a sight to see!

Celebrating the Changing Seasons

With each season's breath, a carnival's glee,
Colors parade like a jubilant spree,
In autumn's embrace, they wear bright hues,
Leaves rustle softly, they sing their blues.

Winter dons a coat, fluffy and white,
While ice crystals sparkle, oh what a sight!
In spring, they burst forth, a lively cheer,
New buds giggle, saying, "Here we are, dear!"

Summer's heat brings a raucous fun,
As leaves dance fervently, basking in sun,
A kaleidoscope of laughter and light,
Frivolities abound from morning to night.

A Carousel of Colors

Round and round the colors spin,
A merry-go-round, they grin and grin,
Golds and reds in a vibrant race,
Twisting together, a dizzying chase.

Pinks and purples join in the fray,
As nature giggles, come join their play,
Whirlwinds of shades catch the eye,
Leaving behind a whimsical sigh.

On this carousel, nothing's amiss,
Every shade sways in a playful bliss,
A riot of hues, a kaleidoscope scene,
In the forest's embrace, all merry and keen!

Dances of Delight Under the Dome

In a grove where laughter weaves,
Leaves wear socks and dance like thieves.
The squirrels cheer, their tails all a-fluff,
As birds chirp jokes, oh, isn't that tough?

When sunlight bounces off the ground,
The shadows jiggle, twist around.
A chipmunk slips, what a funny sight,
He lands in acorns, what pure delight!

A breeze joins in, it's quite a show,
It tickles grass, makes flowers grow.
Even the mushrooms join in the fun,
Swirling in circles, oh what a run!

So come take part in this merry spree,
Where laughter's free, just wait and see.
Under the dome, let joy convene,
In this funny dance, let's be keen!

Garden of the Gleeful

In a patch where giggles bloom,
Tomatoes wear hats, banishing gloom.
Bumblebees buzz with comic flair,
While daisies gossip without a care!

The carrots play hide and seek with glee,
As strawberries chuckle, can you see?
A cabbage rolls, oh what a clown,
With leafy friends, he tumbles down!

The sunflowers wink, donning shades,
While radishes dance in merry parades.
A cucumber slips in a puddle of dew,
Squeaking with joy, falling askew!

From morning 'til sunset, the fun won't cease,
In this garden of laughter, all find peace.
So come and frolic in bright, funny cheer,
Where every plant whispers, joy is near!

Fleeting Moments of Golden Wonder

In golden fields, where laughter flows,
The daisies wiggle, striking a pose.
A dandelion tickles a passing bee,
And whispers softly, 'Just dance with me!'

Clouds tumble by, like fluffy jokes,
As rainbows arch, a choir of folks.
The sun winks bright at the passing breeze,
While rabbits hop in a circus tease!

A butterfly flits, wearing a grin,
Searching for giggles where fun's begun.
An owl's out late, he joins the laugh,
With twinkling eyes, he draws a photograph!

Oh fleeting moments, with laughter we intertwine,
In a world so bright, everything's divine.
Let's capture joy in the golden hour,
With playful hearts, we bloom like a flower!

Cheerful Canopies

Branches stretch wide and sway,
Tickling the clouds in playful ballet.
Squirrels in silly hats jump and slide,
While birds with jokes sing side by side.

Bright sunlight kisses the ground,
Where giggles of children can be found.
A tree that dances with every breeze,
Whispers secrets through rustling leaves.

Beneath its shelter, laughter flows,
As friends exchange silly, secret prose.
Each visit feels like a playful tease,
Where joy is woven through every breeze.

With roots in history, it stands so proud,
Yet it's the quirks that draw the crowd.
In tangled branches, fun does not cease,
This playful giant grants us peace.

When Leaves Sing

When autumn comes with its golden hue,
Leaves start to dance, a show just for you.
Crisp melodies swirl in the light,
As nature's chorus fills the night.

Each leaf a note, a pun of its own,
With shrieks of laughter they are blown.
In the frolic of wind, they prance and play,
Turning every frown into a bouquet.

Dancing twirls make spirits soar,
Whispered giggles behind every door.
Winds weave tales of mirth divine,
In this leafy concert, we all intertwine.

Under the canopy, a stage so grand,
We sway and laugh, holding hands.
Every rustle a joke, every swirl a fling,
Life's a song when the leaves sing.

The Joyful Arborist

A jolly figure with a hefty grin,
Climbs up the tree, where the fun begins.
With pruning shears in one stout hand,
He crafts a playground from this land.

Chasing squirrels who scurry fast,
As laughter mingles with the autumn's blast.
He whispers to critters, tales of delight,
Turn that frown into a beaming sight.

Ropes tied around a sturdy trunk,
He swings like a kid; oh, what a funk!
Each snip of a branch is a giggle set free,
A merry gardener, wild as can be.

When shadows grow long, he calls it a day,
With bark-covered shoes, he dances away.
Echoes of joy in the woods will persist,
Thanks to the folly of the arborist.

Laughter Beneath the Boughs

Underneath boughs where we gather and meet,
Joyful tales echo, oh what a treat!
A picnic sprawled out on a quilt of grass,
With crumbs and giggles, the moments will pass.

Each branch above cradles dreams so bright,
While shadows play games as day turns to night.
From acorns pretending to be tiny hats,
To quick little dances with the neighborhood cats.

We share our snack, we share our smile,
Sipping sweet lemonade, staying awhile.
Nature's own stand-up comedy show,
Leaves spinning tales to let giggles flow.

The sun dips low, but spirits stay high,
Under this healthful canopy, laughter won't die.
For every moment can be pure bliss,
When underneath boughs is where we exist.

Nature's Splendid Revel

In the woods, a dance with glee,
Leaves twirl down from the tree.
Squirrels chase in a silly race,
Nature's laughter fills the space.

Birds in hats, singing bright,
Chirping jokes, what a sight!
Every critter sings along,
Join the chorus, loud and strong!

A fox tries to juggle nuts,
But drops them all, oh such a ruts!
The deer laugh while they leap,
As the woods hold secrets deep.

Breezes join the frolic spree,
Tickling branches with glee.
Dancing shadows, playful cheer,
In this nature's ball of the year.

Joyful Jamboree of Foliage

Amidst the colors, bright and bold,
A merry tale of trees unfolds.
With each gust, the branches sway,
A leafy party on display.

Balloons made from acorn caps,
Squirrels share their silly laughs.
A raccoon in a party hat,
Dances twirls; imagine that!

Wind whispers secrets on the breeze,
As the ground is filled with leaves.
A gathering of laughter and play,
In nature's wild cabaret!

Frogs wear crowns, oh what delight!
As they croak out jokes that night.
Together in this merry throng,
A joyful time, where all belong.

Patches of Cheer Beneath the Pines

Underneath the pines so grand,
Critters gather, hand in hand.
With chuckles and a gleeful shout,
Fun is what it's all about.

A hedgehog tells a funny tale,
As laughter bounces like a hail.
Bunnies hop with giggles bright,
Underneath the pale moonlight.

Chirping crickets keep the beat,
While fireflies dance around our feet.
The bushes shake with merriment,
In this joyful establishment.

Ticklish roots and dancing ferns,
In nature's laughter, joy returns.
Life's a sketch—a cartoon cheer,
In the woods where fun draws near.

Autumn's Raucous Revelry

Leaves are falling, what a scene,
A patchwork quilt of orange sheen.
Frolicking critters lose their minds,
In this festive party of kinds.

Rakes become dance partners, too,
As squirrels swirl in a bright blue hue.
Pumpkins hosting a wacky race,
Cheering loudly in this place.

The owls wearing glasses, quite a show,
Holding court, all aglow.
With every whoot, a wisecrack flows,
As the laughter only grows.

Jumps and tumbles, what a spree,
Nature's own jubilee!
In every rustle, hear the song,
In this crazy world, we all belong.

The Orchard's Whimsy

In a grove where giggles grow,
Apples tell jokes in a row.
They chuckle and dance on the breeze,
Making funny faces with ease.

A squirrel juggles acorns round,
While the sun beams down without a sound.
Leaves tease the wind to come and play,
As critters join in on the ballet.

The branches sway with a silly grin,
Welcoming all who wander in.
Butterflies wear polka-dots bright,
Painting the day with pure delight.

From trees that chuckle, fun takes flight,
A picnic spread, a joyful sight.
In this place, laughter grows thick,
With nature's humor, a perfect trick.

Kaleidoscope of Laughter

Colorful leaves in a swirling dance,
Invite us all to take a chance.
With every twist, bright chuckles rise,
As nature dons its funny disguise.

Beneath the boughs, the shadows play,
Making silly shapes as they sway.
A rabbit hops with a jaunty flair,
While squirrels wear leaves in their hair.

Bright oranges, reds all around,
In this laughter, joy is found.
The sky reflects a giggling hue,
As we join in the laughing crew.

Each step a beat, a playful sound,
In the orchard where smiles abound.
With every rustle, we find our glee,
In this kaleidoscope, so wild and free.

Playful Shadows at Dusk

As daylight fades, shadows stretch wide,
They dance together, side by side.
A funny frog hops with such flair,
Tickling the dusk with its playful dare.

Crickets chirp a silly tune,
While fireflies twinkle, one by one they swoon.
Echoes of laughter bounce through the air,
As time slips by without a care.

The moon peeks out, a grin so bright,
Shining down on the laughter's flight.
Whispers of joy swirl all around,
In this whimsical world, we're spellbound.

So come, let's dance till the stars align,
In the shadows, where our laughter shines.
With each merry step, let's chase away night,
In this playful realm, everything feels right.

Chasing Leaves in a Waltz

Around we spin, in circles of gold,
As leaves break free from branches bold.
They twirl and twist with every gust,
In this waltz of mirth, we must trust.

Silly squirrels, with acorns in tow,
Performing tricks in a row to show.
Their antics make us laugh out loud,
As they prance and leap, so proud.

The ground is a carpet of colors bright,
Each step we take feels so light.
With every rustle, a giggle escapes,
As we chase the leaves in joyful shapes.

Dancing under a sun setting low,
The charm of laughter begins to flow.
In this playful creation, we all find ease,
In golden moments, we chase the breeze.

Leaves that Laugh and Play

In the breeze they twirl and sway,
Little giggles in the fray.
Dancing gently in the light,
Whispering secrets, pure delight.

Tickles from the autumn air,
Joyful rustles everywhere.
Colors bright, a silly sight,
Every leaf a laugh so bright.

Down they fall, a playful tease,
Spinning slowly with such ease.
On the ground, they perform tricks,
Nature's jesters, full of kicks.

As the sun begins to set,
Leaves still laugh, no sign of fret.
Round and round they spin and play,
In the heart of a autumn day.

Nature's Cheerful Chorus

In the woods, a song takes flight,
Birds and leaves harmonize right.
Laughter bubbles through the trees,
Nature sings with every breeze.

Squirrels chatter, doing flips,
Maple branches lend them grips.
The rhythm of the life so grand,
Every creature lends a hand.

Amid the leaves, a prankster lies,
Sticky sap, a sweet surprise.
Friends all gather, giggles flow,
Nature's crowd, putting on a show.

As the sun sets in a blaze,
The choir hums through summer days.
In every rustle, every cheer,
Laughter echoes, loud and clear.

Beneath the Canopy of Joy

Underneath, the antics rise,
Bouncing leaves and playful sighs.
Little shadows dance and play,
All together, come what may.

A jester's hat upon a branch,
Leaves prance around, a lively dance.
Every gust, a burst of glee,
Mirthful whispers, wild and free.

Roots tickle at the ground,
Every creature gathers 'round.
Ants in line, with little haste,
Joining in the joyful feast.

So come and join beneath the shade,
In their games, you won't be swayed.
With every laugh, the heart will soar,
Beneath the canopy, forevermore.

Mischief in the Maple Blooms

In the blooms, mischief brews,
Petal giggles, silly hues.
Dancing pollen all about,
Nature's joy, without a doubt.

Bees buzzing, oh what a scene,
Chasing blooms, so full of sheen.
Maple whirls in sunlit rays,
Mischief spreads through sunny days.

Squirrels hide with nuts concealed,
In this world, laughter's revealed.
Playing tricks on passerby,
In the leaves, a playful spy.

So if you wander, do beware,
Laughter glimmers in the air.
In every bloom and every nook,
Find the joy, just take a look!

Jubilant Journeys in the Glen

In the glen where giggles swirl,
Squirrels dance and ropes unfurl.
Each step a hop, each leap a cheer,
Nature's spirit draws us near.

Bubbles bounce in sunny rays,
Grass tickles in a playful maze.
With every turn, a laugh ignites,
As frolicsome creatures take to heights.

Breezes whisper silly tales,
Of mischievous frogs in leafy trails.
Joy erupts like bursting spring,
In the heart of zestful zing!

Trail of giggles, laughter spread,
In every flower's smile, we're led.
Run with bubbles, skip and roam,
In this glen, we find our home.

Laughter Etched in Leafy Shadows

Amidst the splendor, shadows play,
Leaves chuckle at the light of day.
Branches sway with silly glee,
Echoing joy, wild and free.

Beneath the trees, a gnat takes flight,
Dancing madly, oh, what a sight!
The rhythm of fun is swift and tight,
As critters join the merry rite.

Sunbeams dazzle with a wink,
As blooms and laughter start to sync.
Even the rocks wear silly grins,
While woodland brims with joyful spins.

Here, in shadows, giggles bloom,
Nature's stage, a joyous room.
Amidst the leaves, we're all aglow,
In this realm of laughter's flow.

The Joyous Heart of the Forest

Deep in the woods, where joy resides,
With every step, a laughter rides.
A chipmunk jigs on a fallen log,
Bouncing around like a merry frog.

The mockingbird sings, "What a prank!"
While laughter dances in the tank.
Breezes carry jokes we share,
In this wonder, no room for despair.

Mushrooms giggle with hats so round,
As acorns tumble without a sound.
Every rustle, a tickling tease,
In nature's camaraderie, we're sure to please.

An owl winks from its lofty perch,
With wisdom wrapped in a joyful search.
Here in the heart, we come alive,
Where giggles and chuckles gladly thrive.

Colors That Sing

Colors burst in a vibrant spree,
Splashes of laughter, wild and free.
The petals sway in rhythmic beats,
Nature's joy in sunny feats.

Crimson leaves tell tales of fun,
While golden rays add to the run.
Each hue a laugh, each shade a cheer,
Painting smiles from ear to ear.

The sky a canvas of bright delight,
Where polka-dots twirl, oh what a sight!
With each gust of wind, colors collide,
In this gala of joy, we all abide.

Jubilant tones from the critters' song,
In every corner where we belong.
Together we dance in this lively fling,
In a world where colors sing!

Dappled Sunlight Serenade

Bright patches dance on grass,
A silly squirrel starts to prance.
He chases shadows, quick and spry,
While giggling breezes float nearby.

The branches sway, they clap and cheer,
As sunbeams tickle all that's near.
Each leaf a stage, in playful trance,
With nature's choir in full romance.

A robin croons a cheeky tune,
While ants march by in careful swoon.
They tip their hats, a grand salute,
To all the fun they can't dispute.

Oh, what a show, this bright delight,
With laughter swirling day and night.
In dappled light, all troubles fade,
Join the parade, don't be afraid!

A Symphony in Scarlet

Crimson whispers in the breeze,
As branches giggle, tease with ease.
The hues of autumn's cheeky grin,
Invite the good times to begin.

A jolly jester in a tree,
Hiding acorns cheekily.
With every bounce, a hearty scope,
In this bright world, we find our hope.

Leaves swirl 'round in playful dance,
Nature's jesters take their chance.
A tap, a twirl, a sudden leap,
Into the laughter that's ours to keep.

With every rustle, joy takes flight,
As critters join the grand delight.
A heart so light, we spin and sway,
In scarlet symphony, come what may!

Whirling Twirls of Delight

Leaves spiral down in dizzying flights,
A whirlwind of fun in playful sights.
As children laugh and twirl around,
In every flurry, joy is found.

A chubby chipmunk rolls with glee,
Chasing shadows, wild and free.
While sunbeams frolic, giggle, gleam,
In this whimsical autumn dream.

Twists and turns, oh what a ride,
Nature's dance, a joyful guide.
The air is thick with laughter's call,
As leaves make sure we have a ball.

Whirling curls of bright delight,
In every corner, pure excite.
We're caught in mirth, we skip and sway,
In this ballet that won't decay!

Rustling Secrets of the Grove

In hidden corners, whispers play,
Among the branches, secrets sway.
Curious critters gather 'round,
For tales of joy, where laughs abound.

An owl with spectacles and flair,
Shares stories with a knowing stare.
While foxes giggle at the plot,
The mischief brews, like a bubbling pot.

The rustling leaves share giggly jests,
As nature hosts its merry guests.
From acorns flying left and right,
In this grove of sheer delight.

Underneath the tree so grand,
We share the laughter, hand in hand.
With whispers of joy, we create a trove,
Of rustling secrets in the grove!

Whirlwind of Joyful Tints

In autumn's dance, oh what a sight,
Leaves whirl around, a colorful flight.
They tickle the breeze, with a cheeky grin,
As squirrels scamper, and the laughter begins.

Orange, yellow, and red take their turn,
As if each leaf has a secret to churn.
They twist and they turn, in a grand parade,
Nature's jesters, never to fade.

A gust of wind, they tumble and soar,
Like playful jesters, they beg for encore.
With every rustle, a giggle escapes,
In the whimsical dance, nature's landscapes.

So let's join the mirth, in a leaf-covered spree,
With laughter that flutters, wild and free.
For when the leaves fall, the fun's just begun,
In the joyful ballet, all can join in the fun.

Nature's Glee in a Leafy Embrace

Beneath golden boughs, where shadows play,
A joyous ensemble sways through the day.
Leaves beam brightly, like kids at a show,
In a leafy embrace, they steal the glow.

With each little twirl, they whisper and cheer,
Tickling the branches, without any fear.
Nature's own laughter, bubbling with glee,
As the forest echoes, 'Come join us, whee!'

Caterpillars giggle on branches so tight,
While crickets sing songs deep into the night.
With a rustle and jingle, the forest's alive,
In this leafy embrace, we all smile and thrive.

So let's be merry, oh let's be bright,
In a world where even the leaves feel just right.
Nature's own antics, a festival spread,
In this joyous place, we'll dance till we're fed.

Laughter Trapped in Gossamer Veins

In the heart of the woods, where colors collide,
Laughter is caught in the leaves' merry ride.
Each gossamer vein lends a tickle, a tease,
As whispers of joy float on the breeze.

The sun gives a wink, while shadows then play,
Teasing the branches in a whimsical way.
Every fluttering leaf, a smile in disguise,
A treasure of chuckles beneath azure skies.

Oh, dance with the ferns, spin round with delight,
In nature's own laughter, everything's bright.
As rustling echoes bounce off the trees,
The music of mirth drifts softly on leaves.

So join in the chorus, let your heart sway,
For laughter is waiting, come out and play!
In the lushness of life, let the good times begin,
With joy all around, inside gossamer skin.

A Tapestry of Delight

Stitch by stitch, the colors intertwine,
In a tapestry rich, where merriment shines.
Leaves of all shades weave a tale so grand,
Of laughter unspooling, hand in hand.

A fuchsia leaf twirls with a shimmering gold,
Telling the stories that never grow old.
With giggles and grins, they spin in the air,
A quilt of pure joy, beyond compare.

The branches hold secrets, whispers they share,
As the wind plays its tune, weaving everywhere.
With every flip and flutter, the fun's set in motion,
In this crafty delight, hearts swell like an ocean.

So come gather round, and relish the view,
In this vibrant canvas, there's always room for you.
For a tapestry sewn from nature's own thread,
Wrap up in the laughter, where good vibes are bred.

Sunlit Smiles in September

Golden leaves dance in the air,
Chasing laughter everywhere.
Breezes chuckle through the trees,
Tickling branches, swaying leaves.

Squirrels play hide-and-seek,
Beneath the boughs, they sneak and peek.
Acorns tumble, a nutty spree,
Whirling joys of autumn glee.

Fields of pumpkins, smiles galore,
Winking and grinning, asking for more.
Giggling gourds, they sway and roll,
Harvesting fun, that's the goal!

Sunshine brightens every nook,
Nature laughs; come take a look.
In this season, we all play,
Sharing smiles, come what may.

Echoes of Joy in the Forest

Woodland creatures in a race,
Chirping, twirling, full of grace.
Frogs wearing hats, a silly sight,
Jumping to rhythms, pure delight.

Owls hoot jokes from the tall trees,
While rabbits whisper tales with ease.
Singing songs to the moon's light,
Echoes of laughter fill the night.

Mushrooms laugh in polka dots,
Bouncing to rhythms, tying knots.
Blowing bubbles with tiny glee,
Nature's circus, come and see!

Every path a story tells,
With giggles ringing, joy compels.
In this forest, fun doesn't end,
From leafy realms, happiness sends.

The Happy Harvest of Hues

Crimson apples hang with flair,
Winking at the world with care.
Pumpkin pies are in the air,
Sweet and spicy, nothing rare!

Grinning gourds in every field,
Laughter's bounty is revealed.
With giggles flying on the breeze,
Joyful moments make hearts seize.

Golden corn and colorful beans,
Playful shadows form their scenes.
Frolicking in the autumn sun,
Harvesting laughter, just for fun!

A festival of colors bright,
Chasing away the coming night.
In each bundle, mischief waits,
Smiles abound, for happiness creates.

Whimsy Among the Branches

Bouncing boughs in cheerful sway,
Ticklish twigs, come out to play.
Chirping birds, they tease and taunt,
A raucous party, nature's jaunt!

Dancing leaves in swirling ballet,
Spin and twirl, what a display!
Crazy critters join the fun,
Under the bright and warming sun.

Whimsical whispers through the trees,
Rustling secrets on the breeze.
A twist of vine, a playful vine,
Twirled in laughter, all so fine.

Under the sky, such a sight,
Silly shadows, day and night.
In nature's joy, we find our wings,
Among the branches, laughter sings.

Frivolous Flutters of Autumn

Leaves dance like jesters, in the breeze they twirl,
A whirlwind of colors, in a whirl they unfurl.
They giggle and tumble, like children at play,
While squirrels plot mischief, to snatch them away.

Pumpkins wear smiles, at the harvest parade,
Corn cobs with jokes, in the sunlight they wade.
With every gust, a chuckle takes flight,
As nature dons costumes, a comical sight.

Sipping warm cider, the owls hoot a tune,
While critters all gather, beneath the bright moon.
A chorus of giggles, in rustling attire,
Each moment of autumn, stoked laughter's bright fire.

So join in the revels, let your heart feel the cheer,
For the season of fun is abundantly here.
With breezes that tickle, and joy in the air,
The foliage whispers: let's dance without care.

The Serenade of Swaying Trees

In the grove, the trees wear hats made of leaves,
Swinging to rhythms, as autumn believes.
Boughs bend with laughter, each movement a jest,
While critters and branches join in as a guest.

A squirrel with acorns, a trunk full of glee,
Plays hide-and-seek with a bee on a spree.
The tunes of the forest, all bouncy and bright,
Are sung by the wind in its shimmying flight.

Twisting and turning, the branches compare,
Who dances the best with the soft autumn air.
They chuckle together, a rustling delight,
As shadows and sunbeams invite in the night.

So sway with the trees, let your worries take leave,
In this merriment, everyone can believe.
With every round of whirls, their joy is so free,
A serenade echoing, just you wait and see.

Autumn's Joyful Whispers

Whispers of joy in the soft autumn frost,
Chasing the sun, no moment is lost.
Frolicking leaves, like children they tease,
In the cool, crisp air, they move with such ease.

A raccoon in shades, wearing leaves as a crown,
Sneaks off with an acorn, then trips with a frown.
The sun chuckles low, painting gold on the ground,
While laughter and rustles dance all around.

Clouds wear their puffs like fluffy, white hats,
As critters conspire, their giggles like chats.
Each breeze is a tickle, a playful embrace,
As nature delights in this whimsical space.

So come join the chorus, where mirth's in the air,
In this joyful season, leave behind every care.
For laughter is fleeting, but let it be known,
In autumn's embrace, we are never alone.

Laughter Among the Leaves

Laughter cascades as the leaves take their flight,
Twisting and turning, they dance with delight.
In hidden nooks, where the shadows hold sway,
The chatter of crickets keeps worries at bay.

A scarecrow dons goggles, its hat askew,
Waves at the passers, pretending it's new.
While pumpkins conspire in their bright orange glow,
Sharing old jokes that the harvest winds blow.

With a rustle and shuffle, the branches all sway,
Encouraging giggles to join in the fray.
The ground is a carpet, of colors so neat,
Where critters sing songs that are faintly offbeat.

So come, grab a partner, and dance in the leaves,
For each step is a story that warmly believes.
Embrace the absurd, let joy be the theme,
In this forest of laughter, life's one big dream.

Acorn Antics in the Glen

In the glen where squirrels play,
Acorns fall in wild ballet.
They dance and twirl, oh what a sight,
Chasing tails till the fall of night.

A plump nut rolls, oh what a chase,
One little creature takes first place.
But slips and tumbles down the hill,
Lands in a puddle, full of thrill!

Laughter echoes through the trees,
As critters join with rustling leaves.
A nutty race, what joy they gain,
Nature's jesters, boundless, untamed.

With every leap and silly fall,
The glen bursts forth with laughter's call.
Join the fun, come take a peek,
In this nutty land, the woodland's cheek!

Boughs of Bliss

Boughs adorned with laughter bright,
Swinging critters, pure delight.
Chirping birds play tag in flight,
While branches sway from left to right.

A raccoon dons a silly hat,
Claims a perch, and then falls flat!
Laughter builds as friends all cheer,
For clumsy pals, we always steer.

The breeze brings tales from every nook,
Of mishaps past, each happy look.
In this haven, joy runs free,
Boughs of bliss, a comedy.

Snap a twig, hear the chorus sing,
A symphony of nature's fling.
From tangled vines to laughter's bliss,
Each leafy dance is a playful kiss!

Buoyant Breezes and Bright Hues

Buoyant breezes lift the cheer,
With colors bright, they play here.
Yellow leaves in whirlwinds glide,
Spinning tales with nature's pride.

A fox jumps in a puddle, splashing,
His friends break out in wild dashing.
With every puddle, giggles soar,
And barks arise, who could want more?

Golden hues dazzle in the sun,
A merry dance, oh what fun!
Shade and light, they spin around,
In this realm, joy knows no bound.

As branches sway, the world goes wild,
Each gust of glee embraces the child.
Join the laughter, grab a friend,
In this play, the fun won't end!

Revelations Among the Treetops

Among the treetops, secrets lie,
As whispers of the wind float by.
A koala sneezes with a boom,
Sending leaves to their leafy doom.

An owl hoots, with eyes so bold,
Claims the crown of stories told.
With hidden jokes in every nook,
A zany script, come take a look!

Rabbits giggle at all the fuss,
They paint the grass, without a rush.
With colors bright and brushes free,
Art of laughter, their tapestry.

Under the sun, the fun resumes,
Nature's theater bursts with blooms.
Revel in joy, let spirits soar,
In these high branches, forevermore!

Giggles in the Glade

In the shade where shadows play,
Leaves dance with a cheeky sway,
Squirrels laugh and chase around,
Tickling branches, joyful sound.

Butterflies in colors bright,
Fluttering with pure delight,
Joking with the buzzing bees,
Sharing giggles in the breeze.

Beneath the boughs, a rabbit hops,
Wearing funny little socks,
Each step brings a bouncing cheer,
Nature's pranksters drawing near.

Laughter echoes, hearts so light,
In the glade, all feels just right,
Every rustle brings a grin,
Join the fun; let joy begin!

The Happy Treetops

Up high where the wild birds sing,
Branches sway as the sunlight swings,
Leaves whisper with giggle sounds,
Joyful dance where mirth abounds.

Nutty squirrels strike a pose,
Chasing dreams among the bows,
Breezes tickle those above,
Spreading laughter like a glove.

Nature's clown, the breezy air,
Teases twigs, lifts spirits bare,
Flying high, oh what a sight,
Every moment feels so bright.

Joyful days in leafy crowns,
Mischief sways and never frowns,
Every branch and leaf agree,
Treetops shout, "Just laugh with me!"

Paintbrush of the Wind

A gentle stroke across the green,
Wind laughs, a playful scene,
Tickling leaves with vibrant glee,
Art in motion, wild and free.

Colors swirl where shadows blend,
Nature giggles, never ends,
With each gust, a canvas spins,
Painting joy, the laughter wins.

Branches dance, they twist and sway,
Making merry through the day,
Chattering birds add their tunes,
Sing of fun beneath the moons.

An artist bold, the wind does roam,
Transforming trees into a home,
For giggles born from rustling leaves,
Letting joy in hearts achieve.

Revelry in Rustling Foliage

In the woods, a gathering cheer,
Rustling leaves, all draw near,
Creatures small with tails like whips,
Share their laughter, sweet lip tips.

The foliage knows how to tease,
Shaking giggles with the breeze,
A playful rustle, then a shout,
Nature's party, there's no doubt!

Frogs in hats leap with a grin,
Finding fun that's just within,
Swaying fronds and playful song,
Encouraging all to join along.

So here we sit, in leafy joy,
Every moment, a sweet ploy,
To fill this space with fun's embrace,
In rustling foliage, a happy place.

Festive Fragments of Color

In a garden bright, they giggle and sway,
Dancing on branches, come join the play!
Red cheeks and laughter, a boisterous tune,
They tickle the sunlight, a whimsical boon.

With whispers of orange, they craft silly hats,
Squirrels in comedies, oh how they chat!
Pinecones a'rolling, like marbles they fly,
Creating a circus beneath the blue sky.

Yellow confetti, they sprinkle with flair,
Rustling and chuckling, they're quite the affair.
Each leaf is a jester, a trickster at heart,
In this lively show, camaraderie starts.

When autumn arrives, there's joy all around,
A festival blooms without sound in the ground.
From trees to the earth, they send forth a cheer,
For nature's own laughter is always so near.

Wonderment in the Waving Leaves

Leaves like confetti in brisk autumn breezes,
Their jolly demeanor just never ceases.
One leaf does a flip, another a spin,
With chuckles and giggles, they always win.

A waltz through the park, they're clapping in rows,
Pretending to dance with the wind, oh it flows!
They tug at the branches, a merry parade,
Whirling and twirling, no plans ever made.

Pathways are painted in hues bold and bright,
Each step brings a chuckle, each glance brings delight.
They tease little critters, the birds laugh along,
In the finale, a chorus, nature's grand song.

As twilight sets in, colors fade on cue,
But the laughter lingers, oh how they grew!
They whisper their secrets, a magical tease,
In the heart of the forest, joy rides the breeze.

Portraits of Playfulness in Nature

In the sketch of the woods, a cheeky display,
Leaves glimmer in colors that flip and sway.
They play peek-a-boo with shadows and sun,
A canvas of giggles where all have their fun.

With a swirl of laughter, they scatter like sprites,
Chasing the moonbeams on starry nights.
The branches are trampolines for dreams yet to soar,
Full of mischief, they plot and explore.

So small and so sprightly, they pop in and out,
Crafting a tapestry of whimsy and doubt.
A prankster's delight, they tickle the breeze,
Whisking away worries with each swaying tease.

Their laughter's contagious, you can't help but grin,
In every rustle, there's joy tucked within.
Nature's own jesters, forever they play,
Creating a symphony in their dark leafy way.

A Dance of Amber and Joy

Amber twirls brightly, a dance in the breeze,
Spinning in circles, they jiggle with ease.
Frosty fun winks from underneath ground,
They're planning a party without making a sound.

With each leap and shout, the giggles soar high,
Leaves tumble and tumble, they reach for the sky.
A conga of colors, they shimmy and sway,
In this playful ballet, oh come out and play!

Life's but a sketchbook for all to express,
They scribble their joy, no need to impress.
Nature's own canvas, a palette so bright,
With each dancing leaf, it's pure, pure delight.

As dusk starts to settle, a wink and a sigh,
They fold in their laughter, a soft lullaby.
But soon, they'll return to the dance of the day,
For in each merry moment, they never decay.

Glimmers of Golden Bliss

Under the sun, the branches sway,
Whispers of laughter in bright array.
Squirrels in caps with acorn treats,
Juggling nuts in their tiny feats.

Nature's jesters in costumes bold,
Telling secrets that never grow old.
With every gust, a playful shout,
Leaves burst forth, dancing about.

Joyful colors paint the scene,
Beneath the boughs, a raucous green.
Rabbits skip in a patchwork line,
Gathering treasures as they dine.

The sun bids farewell to day's embrace,
While shadows linger, in quirky grace.
Evening's giggles in twinkling light,
The forest chuckles, happy and bright.

When Leaves Dance to a Tune

In the breeze, a melody flows,
Each rustle a note, as laughter grows.
Twisting and twirling, they sway with glee,
Leaves leap about, wild and free.

A jaunty jig, the branches shake,
While birds chime in, for goodness' sake!
Nature's own band strikes up a song,
With chirps and flutters, they can't go wrong.

Footloose petals in vibrant cheer,
Invite the critters to join them near.
With frolicsome hops and curious spins,
Every dancing leaf just loves to grin!

What fun to witness, this leafy spree,
As they tap their toes with wild esprit.
As dusk descends, the songs do fade,
But echoes of joy will never evade.

Echoes of Playful Breezes

A tickle of wind, a cheeky tease,
Rustling the branches with playful ease.
Whispers of giggles float through the air,
As nature spins tales beyond compare.

With a flutter and flap, the stories unfold,
Of sunbeam adventures, so bright and bold.
Mice in top hats and owls with flair,
Gather round, for stories to share.

A chorus of chuckles from trees so wise,
As shadows play tricks and feign surprise.
Each flicker of light, a punchline found,
In this merry woodland, joy knows no bound.

So come take a stroll where the echoes ring,
Where laughter of nature is the ultimate king.
Through whispers and breezes, let glee be your guide,
In the realm where the fantastical abide.

A Carousel of Colors

Round and round, the hues do spin,
In a game of tag, where to begin?
Crimson and amber in a raucous race,
Each twist and turn brings a new face.

Golden glimmers shine like a crown,
While purples whirl, up and down.
In colorful chaos, the laughter swells,
As autumns' frame their joyful spells.

Each leaf a riot in vibrant glee,
They prance like madmen, dancing free.
With a fuzz and a fizzle, they tumble down,
Joining the carpet of gold on the ground.

The carousel spins while critters cheer,
In a kaleidoscope of fun so clear.
Ever so playful, their colors collide,
A spectacle of joy nature won't hide.

An Ode to the Glorious Foliage

Oh, leafy clown, in colors bright,
You tickle the sky, a comical sight.
With a rustling giggle, you wave and sway,
Dancing in sunshine, come join the play!

Your branches twist, a jester's delight,
Swirling with laughter from morning till night.
In the breeze, you tease, a playful friend,
Fluttering whispers that never suspend.

Golden and crimson, what hues do you wear?
A silly ensemble for all who dare.
With every gust, you spring and you bounce,
A joyful spectacle that makes hearts pounce!

Oh vibrant crown, so full of glee,
You laugh at the storms, wild and free!
In your leafy tavern, jokes never cease,
Under your shade, we all find peace.

Glee on the Wind's Whispers

When breezes hum a playful tune,
Leaves come alive, like a merry balloon.
Swirling and spinning, twirling in flight,
Each gust brings laughter, pure and bright!

Clouds of cotton, in a jesting race,
Chasing the sun, leaving not a trace.
Whispers of joy, they giggle along,
Nature's soft chorus, a whimsical song!

Beneath the branches, secrets take flight,
Squirrels have parties by day, not night.
Up in the crowns, the critters conspire,
Swinging and swapping their dreams, never tire.

So let us dance on this vibrant stage,
With laughter afoot, we turn the page.
In the land of foliage, all troubles cease,
Nature's own humor, a source of bliss.

A Treetop Tapestry of Joy

In a patchwork quilt, leaves start to weave,
A tapestry rich, none would believe.
Pinks, golds, and greens, all in a line,
Each flap and flutter is simply divine!

Squirrels don hats, and acorns parade,
Bouncing around in this leafy charade.
Chirping and chattering, full of delight,
Creating a circus of mischief in sight!

Grass tickles toes as we prance along,
Nature's wild jesters, we hum their song.
We giggle and grin with hearts open wide,
For in these branches, pure joy does reside!

So join the festivities under the sun,
Where laughter and love meld, and joy is spun.
A celebration of life from the tallest of trees,
A giggle-filled dance with the crisp autumn breeze!

Swaying Melodies of the Season

Hear the leaves sing in the joyous air,
A melody flows, light, free and rare.
With each gentle sway, a wink and a grin,
Foliage laughing, let the fun begin!

Rustling and rustling, like giggles they flow,
Nature's own orchestra, delight in tow.
Branches are dancers, performing their art,
Each spin and twirl a song from the heart.

Under the canopy's playful embrace,
Life's little quirks find their perfect place.
A breezy jest, as shadows play tag,
In this seasonal show, no friendly brag!

So rally the joy with friends by your side,
Through the luster of leaves, we'll joyfully glide.
With laughter as music, we celebrate now,
In this merriful grove, we take our bow!

Whimsy in the Woods' Embrace

In a forest of giggles, leaves dance high,
Swaying to laughter as breezes sigh.
Squirrels tell jokes, while acorns jest,
Nature's own circus, a merry fest.

The branches are swinging, a wobbly show,
Beneath them, the rabbits put on a row.
Raccoons in tuxedos slide down on cue,
While a wise old owl hoots, 'What's cooking, crew?'

Moss wears a wig made of bright, sunny cheer,
The ferns tickle toes, bringing giggles near.
Each bark has a chuckle, each leaf a grin,
In this whimsical woodland, the fun won't thin.

So join in the laughter, frolic and play,
Where nature's quirks show in the silliest way.
Let's prance with the pines, engage in their tease,
In this joyous embrace, may we never cease.

The Ecstasy of Nature's Palette

Colors collide in the brightest of schemes,
Each hue a prankster, bursting with dreams.
Goldenrod giggles, and purples unite,
As reds do cartwheels, oh what a sight!

The sunflowers bow with their heads held high,
While daisies spin jokes, oh my oh my!
Butterflies flutter like jesters on wings,
Painting the air with all sorts of flings.

Rain drops play peek-a-boo, what a delight,
Dripping on petals with laughter in flight.
A rainbow rolls in, bursting forth with glee,
An artist of joy in the grand marquee.

Nature's own canvas, so lively and bold,
By hand of the trickster, a story unfolds.
So paint me with laughter, in vibrant embrace,
In this realm of sheer joy, we find our place.

Lighthearted Leaves in a Breezy Waltz

Leaves flutter down, they whisper and sway,
Dancing on air, it's a whimsical play.
Each twist and each turn holds a giggling beat,
As the branches nod on their joyous feet.

The breezes are flirts, teasing while they roam,
Guiding the leaves like they're going home.
With a twirl and a spin, they tumble around,
Creating a ruckus, a delightful sound.

A gust from the north strikes up a new jig,
And the maples respond with a boisterous wig.
They prance and they chuckle, so sprightly and free,
In a bright, breezy waltz, come dance along with me!

So gather your giggles and join in this spree,
With laughter as our rhythm, how joyous we'll be.
In the rustling green, we'll share in the fun,
As lighthearted leaves dance till the day is done.

Echoes of Autumn's Merriment

The rustle of leaves is a chorus so bright,
Singing sweet stories in the soft twilight.
Every crunch underfoot brings laughter back round,
As nature's orchestra plays the best sound.

Pumpkins wear grins with their silly little shapes,
While squirrels jive in their nutty escapes.
Chestnuts and laughter like confetti unfold,
With tales of the woods that are funny and bold.

A breeze brings a giggle, as empires sway,
While shadows join in, in a playful ballet.
With hats made of leaves and scarves spun of vine,
The echoes of autumn are simply divine.

So listen, oh hear, the mirth all around,
In the colors of fall, joy is always found.
Amongst all the chuckles and whimsical sights,
Autumn's sweet echoes bring smiles and delights.

Whispering Woods of Happiness

In a grove where giggles grow,
Trees tell tales that giggle low.
Squirrels dance in twirls and spins,
While owls chuckle at their wins.

Leaves all rustle, playing pranks,
In nature's playground, wild and frank.
Bunnies hop, wearing silly hats,
As foxes sing in chorus with rats.

The sun peeks through, a warm delight,
Painting shadows, bringing light.
A whimsical breeze takes a twist,
And whispers secrets that can't be missed.

Oh, what joy in every nook,
In this playful, laughing book.
The woods echo with delight and cheer,
In this happy realm, there's nothing to fear.

The Joyful Canopy

Up above, the branches sway,
With leaves that giggle all the day.
Critters join in merriment,
Creating laughter, heaven-sent.

The sunlight bounces, skips around,
As playful shadows dance on ground.
Each rustling leaf, a hearty joke,
In this lively, laughing cloak.

Birds in feathers, all askew,
Chirp out rhymes, just for you.
While squirrels plot a nutty scheme,
In the canopy, it's all a dream.

From dawn till dusk, the fun don't cease,
Nature's jesters find their peace.
Joy flows here like the stream nearby,
In a world where giggles fly.

Children of the Forest

Little faces swirling by,
Chasing shadows, oh so spry.
In the glen, they find their glee,
Among the roots and dancing trees.

They play games of hide and seek,
Where every tree becomes a peek.
Laughter bubbles like a brook,
In the heart of this storybook.

With wildflowers in their hair,
They spin and twirl without a care.
Nature's giggles, a joyful sound,
Echo in the merry ground.

Every child's a forest friend,
In this laughter that won't end.
Through the trees, their joy cascades,
Creating memories that never fade.

Mosaic of Merriment

In a patchwork of colors bright,
Joy pops up in sheer delight.
Every step brings a playful jolt,
As laughter swirls like a waltz.

Tickle the ground, a leaf or two,
Nature grins in every hue.
With every petal, every twig,
There's a giggle, a dance, a jig.

Waving branches high and low,
Invite all to join the show.
Where sunshine spills like warm hot tea,
And every heart beats wild and free.

Woven smiles upon the trail,
Every moment tells a tale.
In this patchwork, joy's alive,
Forever here, we laugh and thrive.

Giggles on the Ground

Leaves fell down like chuckling friends,
Dancing lightly where the breeze bends.
Squirrels play tag, with nuts in hand,
Their prancing steps make laughter land.

Pumpkins grin with crooked smiles,
Cartwheeling raccoons, oh what styles!
The ground is tickled, spins abound,
Joyful echoes all around.

Underfoot the colors burst,
Yellow and orange, a silly thirst.
Nature's cheer, a slapstick show,
As clumsy critters steal the flow.

Bouncing balls of fluff take flight,
Chasing shadows till the night.
Giggles twirl in autumn's voice,
A grand parade, a merry choice.

Celebrations in the Canopy

Branches sway in a merry jig,
Each leaf dressed in festive rig.
Birds compete with silly tunes,
As laughter spills beneath the moons.

Acorns drop like tiny drummers,
Creating beats like joyful summer.
Squirrels swing from branch to branch,
In this forest-wide, funny dance.

Beneath the sky, a confetti rain,
Nature's party, no time for pain.
Fluttering wings in wild delight,
Carrying whispers of the night.

With each gust, the branches sway,
Echoes of mischief, come what may.
High above where chuckles soar,
Nature's jokes forevermore.

Moonlit Revels in Red

Under the glow of a silvery light,
Crickets sing, adding to the delight.
Red leaves twirl with a joyful spin,
As night creatures join the din.

Beneath the stars, shadows sneak,
A fox in pajamas starts to peek.
The moon chuckles, a playful sight,
Illuminating laughter's flight.

In the woods, a feast is spread,
With funny hats atop each head.
Bats swoop down for a comic spree,
Creating silhouettes so carefree.

Smirking owls hold court to chat,
Chasing each other—what's wrong with that?
In every corner, the fun imbues,
As giggles bounce in the midnight hues.

The Spirit of Autumn Radiates

Joy erupts as leaves turn bright,
A raucous glee, a childish sprite.
Pumpkin patches hide and seek,
Laughter booms, a cheerful squeak.

Gathered round the flaming fire,
Tales of chases never tire.
Marshmallows toast with silly burns,
A funny tale, each twist that turns.

In pumpkin hats, kids prance about,
Cracking smiles with every shout.
Wobbly steps on paths they tread,
In this season, joy is spread.

As autumn breezes paint the skies,
Nature revels with merry sighs.
Each leaf a joke, each breeze a grin,
In this light-hearted world we spin.

www.ingramcontent.com/pod-product-compliance
Lightning Source LLC
Chambersburg PA
CBHW051634160426
43209CB00004B/637